HOW TO WRITE A NON-FICTION BOOK IN 30 DAYS

35 Strategic, Foolproof Steps to Get Your Manuscript Complete

By Frances Vidakovic

COPYRIGHT

AUTHOR'S NOTE:

All rights reserved. No part of this book may be reproduced in any manner whatsoever or by any means, electronic, mechanical, photocopying, recording or otherwise, without prior permission from the author, except in the case of brief quotations embodied in critical articles and reviews.

Copyright © 2016 Frances Vidakovic

Frances Vidakovic asserts the moral right to be identified as the author of this work.

CONTENTS

1. Introduction
2. Six Famous Novels Written In Under a Month
3. Proving It Can Be Done – NaNoWriMo
4. Why Writing a Non-Fiction Book Is Infinitely Easier Than Completing a Novel
5. Now Tell Me: How Do You Eat An Elephant?
6. So Why Write A Book In The First Place?
7. Caution: Beware the Companion Who Is About To Start Pestering You
8. Quotes To Keep In Mind When You Need Additional Backup
9. An Alternative Suggestion
10. Another Warning: You Don't Have To Have All The Answers Right Now
11. Now That You Have Your WHY, It's Time To Work Out Your WHAT
12. Plan A
13. Plan B
14. Let's Work Out Your Goals
15. When 1 & 2 Collide
16. Moving Forward
17. Research Is Your Best Friend

18. It's Time To Work Out Your Working Title
19. Chapter Outline
20. The General 30 Day Plan
21. Obvious Things To Keep In Mind
22. Working Out WHEN You Will Write
23. Create A Writing Schedule
24. Find A Good Working Environment
25. Make Sure You Regularly Back Up Your Work
26. Okay I Have A Plan – So How Do I Start Writing?
27. Find Your Voice
28. When You Get Stuck For Ideas
29. Other Writing Tips
30. Avoid These Top 10 Writing Mistakes
31. Get Support From Fellow Writers
32. Useful Writing Tools
33. Summarizing The Most Important Points
34. Writing Quotes To Spur You On
35. In Conclusion

1. Introduction

I want to start this book by saying that what I am proposing to you isn't a preposterous idea. That is, the idea of writing a non-fiction book in 30 days.

I know it isn't impossible because I have done it myself. In fact, I have written many books within 30 days, back to back.

Writing multiple books back to back is not something I would encourage anyone to do because it is truly draining. I felt like I was running on empty after publishing 8 books during 2016.

Instead I share this information with you so that you know it is POSSIBLE.

There is this crazy mentality in society (**especially among** wanna-be writers) that writing a book is HARD. They make it sound as if it is something comparable to running a marathon.

Sure, in some ways it is difficult. You need determination, endurance and a willingness to work hard to finish a book.

However, given that I can barely run two kilometres (I love walking, running not so much!) yet still have 18 books under my belt, I would propose that writing is a lot easier than crossing the finish line after running 42 kilometres straight.

To write your book in 30 days you need to understand that your biggest challenge will be your mindset.

You need to know it isn't impossible or hard.

This goal is in fact achievable.

It has been done many times before (I will provide concrete examples in the next chapter).

To help you do the same, I will provide you with a concrete structure and plan in this book to replicate the same process I have followed many times already.

2. Six Famous Novels Written In Under A Month

Now before you say that I am a freak of nature for being able to write super-fast, I want to show you a few examples of successful books that were also written in under a month.

While these authors weren't necessarily working under a deadline of 30 days, they still achieved what many people say isn't achievable. Once again, these people were proved wrong.

The Boy in the Striped Pyjamas by John Boyne

Irish novelist Boyne was so wrapped up in this tale of a boy living through the Holocaust that he couldn't stop writing it.

He wrote the entire book in two and a half days, barely stopping to eat or sleep throughout the process. It is now a contemporary classic.

On The Road by Jack Kerouac

After seven years on the road, travelling across America and taking notes along the way, Kerouac penned the book, which inspired an entire generation, in only three weeks.

Interestingly, he typed the entire draft on one 120 foot long piece of teletype paper that he taped together before writing.

A Study in Scarlet by Arthur Conan Doyle

The first novel to feature the legendary Sherlock Holmes took only three weeks to write in 1886. This was also the first Sherlock Holmes story to be adapted into film.

The Tortoise and the Hare by Elizabeth Jenkins

In 1954, Jenkins wrote this tale in three weeks after having an affair with a man who refused to leave his wife.

The Gambler by Fyodor Dostoyevsky

The Russian author wrote this tale in 26 days while also writing *Crime and Punishment*.

At the time he was heavily in debt due to his gambling addiction. He decided to quickly write his semi-autobiographical novella as a good way to help him pay off his debts.

The Prime of Miss Jean Brodie by Muriel Spark

Muriel Spark wrote this novel about a fictionalized version of her teacher, Christiana Kay, in only one month.

She said the story was inspired by a 1960 class assignment: "We were given to write about how we spent our summer holidays, but I wrote about how [my teacher] spent her summer holidays instead. It seemed more fascinating."

A Clockwork Orange by Anthony Burgess

Burgess admits writing his best known novel in about three weeks, purely for the purpose of making money. It went on to be adapted by Stanley Kubrick.

As I Lay Dying by William Faulkner

Faulkner wrote his masterpiece in less than six weeks while working the night shift at a power plant. He also amazingly claims he didn't change a single word.

I, the Jury by Mickey Spillane

Spillane wrote his Mike Hammer novel in nine days – impressive given the book went on to sell 7 million copies in three years.

IT TOOK A TAD LONGER THAN A MONTH BUT STILL…

Casino Royale by Ian Fleming

Fleming's first Bond novel took approximately two months to write. Each of his following Bond novels took even less - about six weeks apiece.

The Confidential Agent by Graham Greene

Greene was writing his career-defining masterpiece, *The Power and the Glory*, when he decided to write another novel to make some money. *The Confidential Agent* was written in six weeks.

A Christmas Carol by Charles Dickens

Here's another beloved classic that was written in a remarkably short amount of time. *A Christmas Carol* took six weeks and came to define the spirit of the season.

King Solomon's Mines by H Rider Haggard

This instant best-seller was written in six weeks in 1885 after a bet that Haggard could write a better tale than Stevenson's Treasure Island. (Yes, a little bit longer than a month but still an amazingly quick time!)

3. Proving It Can Be Done - NaNoWriMo

In case you haven't heard of this challenge, NaNoWriMo is short for National Novel Writing Month. This is an annual, internet-based creative writing project which takes place during the month of November.

During NaNoWriMo, participants are challenged to write a 50,000 word manuscript between November 1 and November 30 of every year.

This challenge started back in 1999 as a motivational stunt for a small group of writers. It has since become a non-profit organisation with staff, sponsors, and over 100,000 contestants each year.

The rules are simple. Participants must write an average of approximately 1667 words per day in November, to reach the target goal of 50,000 words written towards a novel.

The aim is to get people to start writing, using the deadline as inspiration and incentive to get their story down as words onto paper.

Technically a novel is a lot more than 50,000 words so the participant will usually need more time to complete their book.

But that's okay. The most important thing is that the writers have a head-start, a push, something to spur them into action.

To become a successful writer and get your book complete, it is all about taking action.

4. Why Writing a Non-Fiction Book Is Infinitely Easier Than Completing A Novel

This is where I give you some good news. The goal of this book is to help you write a **non-fiction** book, which is SO MUCH EASIER than writing a novel.

I say this from experience because I have personally written five novels, each with a word-count of approximately 100,000 words.

The quickest amount of time that I was able to complete the majority of these books was six months. Back then, I wrote 20,000 words per month x 5 months. I then took an additional one month to go over everything with a fine-tooth comb and make the appropriate amendments.

But guess what? Non-fiction books don't need to be 100,000 words! In fact, if your non-fiction book is that long you may be doing something wrong. (Or writing something that you could split up into a few different books).

Yes, there are a few wordy non-fiction books around. Yet for the most part, non-fiction books are best when they are short, succinct, to-the-point and focused.

When it comes to non-fiction books, adding fluffy material or rambling on and on for the sake of increasing the word count, is both unnecessary and works to your detriment.

Let me repeat this one more time because it is so important for you to understand:

You need to keep your non-fiction book to the point and cut out all the fluff.

Our goal here is to write 20,000 words for your non-fiction book.

Yes, 20,000 words!

If you would like to write and publish a non-fiction book, 20,000 words is a perfectly acceptable amount, especially when published digitally.

Non-fiction digital books (those published for Kindle for example) sell best when they are easy to read and provide quality content that is easy to digest.

Of course, the length of the average non-fiction book does vary. You will find successful books published with a word count of only 10,000 words and anything up to 50,000 to 70,000 words (and more!).

However a word count of 20,000 words is not only acceptable, it is also very achievable to write in one month. So that is the goal we are aiming for!

5. Now Tell Me: How Do You Eat An Elephant?

We eat it one bite at a time.

I'm sure you have heard this famous saying before. When it comes to dealing with any large task, goal or project, the best way to tackle it is by breaking it into smaller steps. You need to focus on these smaller bites, taking one step at a time.

So how do we break up 20,000 words? It's simple. You write 1,000 words written over 20 days.

That is, 5,000 words a week, allowing yourself the weekends to .review your material, do a quick edit and consolidate your ideas.

Let's do the math: 5000 words x 4 = 20,000 words in a month. 20,000 words = one complete non-fiction manuscript at the end of the 30 days. This is the formula I followed to write each of my non-fiction books.

(*Except for two of them – WHEN HE'S A KEEPER and THEY SAY I'M SPECIAL. Both books took **a lot** longer and ended up with a* *much higher word count because I hadn't at that point worked out this simple formula.)*

If you are a blogger, you most likely write blog posts which average 1,000-2,000 words. Consider this book a compilation of 10-20 blog posts.

If you were ever a college student, you most likely wrote lots of 1,000-2,000 word essays back in the day. Consider this book a compilation of 10-20 essays.

Except this isn't going to be painful like a school assignment that you wish you didn't have assigned to you. Instead, you will write about something YOU ARE EXCITED to write about. You will pick a topic that interests you – something that you love and WANT to write about.

This process will be much like that of giving birth (my apologies to my male readers for this analogy but it is true!)

There will be times during the writing month that you feel uncomfortable and pushed to your limits. But if you stick with the process, you will ultimately give birth to something you love and are proud of. It will be your little baby, your legacy, something you and others can treasure forever.

6. So Why Write a Book In The First Place?

To do anything successfully in life, you need to have a WHY.

Why do you want to push yourself to write a book?

What is the purpose of you writing it?

Honestly, ask yourself WHY you want to accomplish this goal.

Some people seek the instant credibility it can add to their career. When you write a book, you establish yourself as an expert in your field.

Some people write a book to use as a promotional tool for their business. It is the perfect and most impressive business card you can give someone.

Others have a message or ideas that they want to share with others. Writing a book provides them with the opportunity to help others learn more about this topic.

Some see it as a chance to express their creativity, while others see it as a challenge they want to master. They want to prove to themselves and others that they can do anything when they put their minds to it.

Me personally? I don't write for the recognition or fame or accolades or anything like that.

I write because I must. I cannot NOT write.

Whenever I get a grand idea for a book, I know I have to act upon it or the idea will keep bugging and pestering me night and day.

It honestly feels like I have a book inside me, bursting to get out. So I purge my ideas onto paper, out of fear that not doing so might drive me crazy. To be honest, I haven't officially tested out this "driving me crazy" theory because for now, I keep honouring the book ideas that come to mind…

Plus I have two children and a family I adore. I love the notion that a book can exist as my legacy long after I am gone. My family can hold something tangible in their hands and know it is something I created.

I pour my heart and soul into every book I write. I love that my family will be able to read my words in the years to come and still feel my presence there. Or maybe it is more like my ESSENCE, I don't know.

We will all have a different WHY and that is okay. You need to identify what yours is so that you can turn to it during moments of frustration (because they will come). And when you feel like throwing in the towel (expect a few of those days too).

7. Caution: Beware the Companion Who Is About To Start Pestering You

Before we move on to talk about WHAT you are planning to write, I want to assure you that it is NORMAL to feel overwhelmed by the idea of writing a book.

It is normal to not know exactly what your book will look like in the end, at the start of your journey.

Even though you may see a distant light at the end of the tunnel, there will be lots of darkness along the way. Sometimes you will only see the next step you can take.

There's a great chance too that fear will take a walk alongside you on this journey. Fear of failure, fear of success, fear of not being good enough, fear of taking action, fear of .... (You can fill in the blank because chances are you will create or come up with your own personal psychological fears or barriers during this process).

Now I hope the next piece of advice I have for you doesn't offend you (I apologise if it does!) To be honest I can't believe I am even writing this down but here goes:

During your 30 days of writing, you will need to stick your middle finger up at your fear companion.

I hate to say it but he or she may never go away. He may spend the 30 days breathing down your neck or whispering lies into your ear.

He will try to wear you down with his relentless persistence. He will try to trick you into giving up because he doesn't like leaving his comfort zone or going places he has never gone before.

Be aware that this is going to happen. This knowledge means you can prepare in advance for its arrival. So you won't be surprised when it starts jumping up and down in front of you like a crazy person, trying to get your attention.

You must at all times need to stay strong. Keep your eyes forward and focused and learn to ignore that invisible ghost. Don't feed the monster!

This may be your biggest challenge during the month so when he or she starts wearing you down, do what I told you to do. Remember to stick your middle finger up.

8. Quotes To Keep In Mind When You Need Additional Backup

There is only one thing that makes a dream impossible to achieve: the fear of failure. Paulo Coelho

Never give up on a dream just because of the time it will take to accomplish it. The time will pass anyway. Earl Nightingale.

Don't be afraid to fail. Be afraid not to try. Michael Jordan

Everything you want is on the other side of fear. Jack Canfield

It always seems impossible until it's done. Nelson Mandela.

Never give up, for that is just the place and time that the tide will turn. Harriet Beecher Stowe

What is the point of being alive if you don't at least try to do something remarkable? John Green

9. An Alternative Suggestion

Before I move on to the next tip I want you to consider a way of looking at fear as your friend.

By fear, I don't mean fear of failure or success or the other ones that only exist to tear you down.

By fear, I mean the other, more positive type. This is the fear of staying stuck in the same place, the fear of not achieving your dreams and letting your life waste away.

Why not learn to use this fear as a kick-up-the-butt strategy to keep you moving, when you feel like giving up? You want to write a book so why not write it now, when you have the desire and tools to do so?

What is the point of waiting another month or year? Dreams don't just fall into your lap; you need to work hard to chase them.

When you fall down, you need to get up. When you fall down again, you need to brush your knees and continue on.

Expect hurdles and roadblocks along the way. They are a part of life and will pop up whenever you are attempting to achieve something special.

They are a test and the way you pass these tests is by refusing to give up. Do whatever you can to find a way around them.

10. Another Warning — You Don't Have To Have All the Answers Right Now

It is important to mention this now, before we get into the nitty-gritty, because some of you may still overwhelmed by the idea of writing a book. Not because of fear but because you can't see how this will all fall into place together.

Maybe you have an idea but can't imagine what you will write about for 20,000 words.

Or perhaps you *do* have a more concrete plan but aren't sure whether there is enough material to fill a whole book.

Let me assure you by stating that this is how every author starts off feeling.

As I mentioned earlier, it is normal to not know exactly what your book will look like in the end, at the start of your journey.

Some of the magic in focused-writing-with-a-deadline comes from the amazing things that appear out of nowhere when you immerse yourself in this process.

You need to have faith that if you stick to this plan and don't allow procrastination or fear to get in your way, the ideas will come to you.

I have personally found this to be true, when writing both my fiction and non-fiction books.

I didn't ever bother stressing about what my entire manuscript would look like in the end. Instead I woke up each day and tried to think about what I would write for my 1000 words. Just the 1000 words – that was my focus.

When you do your first practice run, you will discover how simple and manageable it is to write 1000 words. It is 10 blocks of 100 words.

You may find that eventually you can whip this amount out quickly, but don't worry if it takes you longer. When I first started writing, 1000 words would take me hours and hours. But over time, this length of time decreased with practice.

When you eliminate the all stress and worry about the ultimate finished product - and instead focus intently on each 1000 words - you will discover that the ideas flow so much easier than you ever expected.

It doesn't matter if you don't know what you are writing about tomorrow. It doesn't matter if you can't imagine what your manuscript will look like in a week or a fortnight.

Don't let that stuff stress you out or crowd your mind with worry.

Focus on today - just today.

Your goal is to write only 1000 words – no more than that is required unless you truly can't help yourself.

Most mornings you may wake up and have no idea what you will write about that today – that's okay. It happened to me all the time (like literally almost every day!) but because I was determined to write those 1000 words, without fail, the material always came to me.

Amazing things start to happen when you stay focused on this goal of 1000 words. You will begin to tap into this weird magic mountain of creative inspiration when you start writing every single day without fail. The words will seem to come to you out of nowhere.

Trust me, it will happen. Don't get in the way of this process by overthinking or worrying about things. Clear your mind, focus on the goal for that day – 1000 words – and get to work on creating something special.

11. Now That You Have Your Why, It's Time to Work out Your WHAT

If you know exactly what you want to write your book about, that's great! Three cheers for you!

I still encourage you to read the following points because it may prove to be useful when it comes to brainstorming ideas.

HOW TO WORK OUT WHAT TO WRITE ABOUT

No doubt the fact that you have purchased this book means the idea of writing a non-fiction book has crossed your mind (obviously!).

So what is that idea?

Is it a little spark of inspiration that you still need to elaborate on or something more solid and concrete?

Do you already have a plan or are you starting from scratch?

Whatever the case, you are in safe hands because I have an exercise for both scenarios.

If you already have an idea, you will need to clarify these thoughts and work out whether there is enough "meat" there to fill a book, without adding unnecessary "stuffing".

I call this vital step Plan A and it should take you only 5 minutes to complete.

If you have zero ideas for a book and feel confused about what to write about (too many ideas, not enough clarity), you will need to jump across to Plan B first.

Once you have completed this Plan B exercise and have made a decision what to write about (don't worry, it will be easier than you suspect), you will return to Plan A and get back on track.

12. Plan A

PLAN A – WHEN YOU HAVE A LITTLE BIT OF AN IDEA WHAT YOUR BOOK WILL BE ABOUT

So you have an idea? If that's the case, I want you to get out a timer and pen and paper right now. You will have exactly five minutes to write down all the ideas you have for your book.

Now we won't be getting into the finer details here yet. Simply write down the general big points you aim to cover in your book. Think of these more like chapter headings or the most important notions that you need to address.

NOTE: THIS ISN'T A TEST. YOU CAN'T FAIL IT!

This exercise is simply getting you to purge all the ideas you have onto paper.

By way of example, I will now choose a random topic and see what I can come up with within five minutes. (Honest to goodness, I'm picking a topic I have never considered writing about before. Let's see where I can go with it!)

The time starts now!

MY RANDOM BOOK IDEA:

HOW TO KEEP YOUR SANITY AS A PARENT

(Ooh this sounds like something I may want to write about!)

MY IDEAS: TIMED 5 MINUTE PURGE

- How to minimise sibling rivalry
- The importance of having mommy time-out
- How to improve communication with your kids
- What exactly drives us crazy?
- How to reduce stress
- Having the right mindset
- Letting go of our need for perfection
- Sane versus insane parenting examples
- Keeping everything in perspective
- Why you should cut yourself some slack

- Tips to keep you sane
- What to do when you feel like you are going crazy
- Parenting gone wrong examples
- Why parenting is the hardest job around

It took me only a few minutes to come up with these ideas, for a topic that randomly crossed my mind. These are all topics that I can elaborate upon further to become chapters in a book.

Now I want you to do the same. Set the timer and write down everything that comes to mind when you think about what needs to be covered in your book.

Whatever you come up with will serve as an initial roadmap of ideas. This can be added to at a later date as you continue to research and develop your rough idea.

This is pretty much the first step in the process of writing and it is fairly simple, right?

If you are stuck for a book idea I want you to proceed to Plan B and come back to Plan A once you have chosen something you think you would like to work on.

13. Plan B

PLAN B – WHEN YOU HAVE A ZERO IDEA WHAT YOUR BOOK WILL BE ABOUT

If you are feeling stuck about your book idea, I want you to start here.

The truth is you probably **do** have an inkling of an idea about what areas interest you the most. For me, I have three main loves that pique my interest.

They are as follows:

- Writing
- Parenting
- Self-development

These are the topics I am most drawn to writing about. When it comes to writing blogs, the ideas that come to my mind always fall into one of these categories.

But you of course may be interested in something completely different.

Here is a list of the most popular book categories that books are written about (according to Amazon):

- Arts and photography
- Biographies and memoirs
- Business and money
- Children's books
- Comics and graphic novels
- Computers and technology
- Cookbooks, food and wine
- Crafts, hobbies and home
- Education and teaching
- Engineering and transportation
- Foreign language
- Health, fitness and dieting
- History
- Humour and entertainment
- Law
- Medical

- Parenting and relationships
- Politics and social sciences
- Reference
- Religion and spirituality
- Science and math
- Sports and outdoors
- Travel

Under each of these categories you will find many subgenres. For example, under parenting (which is something that interests me), you can find books on the following topics:

- Childcare
- Child Development
- Parenting babies and toddlers
- School-age children
- Parenting emotions and feelings
- Motherhood
- Fatherhood
- Adoption
- Special needs parenting
- Parent and child relationships

- Step-parenting and blended families
- Aging parents
- Family activities
- Fertility

For the record, these are only a handful of the suggested sub-genres under the broader umbrella of parenting. I mention it so that you realise that even general topics can be broken down into lots of more niche ideas.

Now before we explore these more specific ideas, I want you to get the timer out and spend five minutes thinking about all the things you would like to write about.

ONCE AGAIN THERE ARE NO RIGHT OR WRONG ANSWERS HERE

Even if you THINK you have no idea, I want you to do the task anyway. This is simply an opportunity to note all the subjects you imagine you might like to write a book about.

Actually, rather than saying "like to write about" I want to change that wording to "LOVE". Think about what you would LOVE to write about.

I say LOVE because I think that having a strong desire and interest in the subject is the magic key that gets you over the finish line. There is nothing worse than spending time researching and writing about a topic that you find tedious and boring (but more about that in the next chapter!)

Complete Plan B now and see what you come up with! Are any of the ideas more viable or exciting than others? It is okay if your ideas are messily scribbled down or don't make any sense. We will make sense of them later.

Once you have identified a few keys areas, I want you to do back and complete the exercise Plan A. Do it for each different idea (shouldn't be too hard as the exercise is only five minutes long!)

END RESULT:

You should now have a rough idea of some potential book ideas. Once this is done, we can proceed to the next chapter.

14. Let's Work Out Your Goals

At this point all you will have is an initial sketch of either one or many book ideas scribbled onto paper.

Some will seem viable, others maybe not so much.

Before we proceed to finalising a book idea, I want to let you know that you have two main options when it comes to writing your non-fiction book. You can either:

1) Go with a passion project or
2) Choose something you are hoping will be profitable and saleable in the end.

By passion project, I mean something that you work on that gives you satisfaction, happiness and meaning in your life. It is a topic you want to write about, even if no one cares to read it later on.

When you write this passion project book, you are not necessarily aiming for it to be a bestseller. Some might not have that desire at all. Instead, you are following a dream you feel you are destined to fulfil. It is a vision that is yours alone.

The second alternative option is to write a book that you are planning to sell.

Maybe it is to support your career. For example, you may be a financial advisor who wants to write a book on your own unique take on financial planning.

Or perhaps you have a new perspective on health and dieting that you believe would be an instant hit. Either way, you are hoping to have it professionally published in the future.

Let's start with the good news about PASSION PROJECTS

With a passion project, you can write whatever you like, without worrying too much about whether it will hit number 1 on the bestseller charts.

This does not mean I will allow you to write 20,000 words of rubbish!

As a writer, who wholeheartedly respects the value of a book, I will still encourage every reader here to write content that flows well, has proper structure and as free from errors as possible.

However, writers of passion project books do have more freedom in their writing because they don't have to abide by the same expectations and rules that published authors do.

They write straight from the heart because they aren't worried so much about judgement from the general public. They do not have to please anyone except themselves.

Now for the BAD NEWS about passion project books

There is no bad news! Write away!

The GOOD NEWS about writing a non-fiction book that you can later publish

The best news is you can do this!

Long gone are the days when writers would send out manuscripts to publishers and wait months to receive a reply (usually a standardised rejection slip in the post!).

It is easier now than ever to have a published good, mainly thanks to Amazon who have revolutionised the digital book market.

With Amazon's self-publishing services you can instantly reach millions or readers worldwide and keep control of your work.

Not only can you independently publish your digital book with Kindle Direct Publishing, it is also fast and simple to publish your book in print with CreateSpace (who are owned by Amazon) and create an audiobook with ACX.

So have faith! Once you have completed and re-edited your draft, there is a star in the horizon (in the form of a hard-copy book) and it has your name on it. You can do it!

Now here's the BAD NEWS about writing a non-fiction book that you can later publish

If you are writing a book you plan to publish, you should know upfront that the expectation is higher when it comes to quality presentation (in terms of book content and the final book cover) than when you publish for personal purposes (in that scenario you only need to please yourself!)

But you knew that would be the case, right?

I'm not telling this news to scare you but so that you can aim for high quality content right from the start.

You will NOT be able to get away with poor research, poor writing, no structure and frequent spelling and grammatical errors as a published author.

That is why you should be aiming for high quality content now (which I know you can do!) High quality content comes from sharing all your best and most important tips/points/advice/findings and leaving out the unnecessary fluff.

Oh and for the record please know that once your 20,000 word draft is complete (by following the tips in this book); there's no rule that says you have to publish your book straight away.

Even though it is outside the scope of this book (my goal is to get the 20,000 words written!), you can take your time preparing the final manuscript. You don't need to rush the editing or formatting of the content or the design of the book cover. You can ultimately publish a book when you feel that it is at the highest standard you deem possible.

Once again, don't stress because I know you can do it!

15. When 1 & 2 Collide

Before moving on, I wanted to mention that there is a third option when it comes to writing a non-fiction book.

That is:

PASSION PROJECT + PUBLICATION

There is no reason why you can't publish your Passion Project and make it profitable.

Some writers do write non-fiction books that they aren't passionate about, purely as a money-making tool. Others pour their hearts out onto paper, hoping it will kept private among family and friends.

Then there is the baby of these two options, when love and potential profitability collide.

I mention this now, after you have completed either the Plan A or Plan B exercise (or possibly both) because I didn't want to confuse your initial ideas with the idea of making money.
I wanted you to get your ideas onto paper, purge it all out, see what was on your mind before you started to analyse it.

Look at what you wrote down. Did these ideas come from your heart or mind (or possibly both)?

In the end, it doesn't matter to me what you choose to write. What matters to me is that you are motivated enough to write it!

As I mentioned before, it helps immensely when you enjoy what you are writing about. If you are writing with view to publication, do at least try to find a topic you love or are passionate about.

Or if it's a boring subject but you still think it's a potentially marketable book, see if you can make it fun.

Working hard for something you don't care about is called stress while working hard for something you love is called passion.

Whatever reason you are writing for, remember these important points:

- ❖ Nothing worth having comes easy.
- ❖ We are what we repeatedly do. Excellence therefore is not an act, but a habit (Aristotle).

- You'll never change your life until you change something you do daily. The secret of your success is found in your daily routine. (John C. Maxwell).

- Focus on your goal. Don't look in any direction but ahead.

- Believe in yourself and you will be unstoppable.

- The most effective way to do it is TO DO IT. Amelia Earhart.

16. Moving Forward

So by this point you have a gist of something you could write a non-fiction book about. What now?

I am going to start by telling you the way I wrote my books.

You already know that the key is to write 1000 words a day over 20 days (using the weekends to catch-up, rest, brainstorm or revise) but what are you going to write about?

The best way to work out your content is to structure and segment your book into smaller parts.

My non-fiction titles to date include:

- ❖ *Do Something! The No-BS Guide for Anyone Who Needs To Stop Wasting Their Time Today*
- ❖ *Inspiring Teens: A Guide to Living Life without Regret*
- ❖ *Life is An Experiment: 100 Experiments to Change Your Life*

- *Life Skills: 100 Things Every Kid Needs To Know before Leaving Home*
- *Lightbulb Moments: 50 AHA! Insights That Will Transform Your Life*
- *Happy Thoughts: 200 Inspiring Quotes Explained for Kids and Teens*
- *Life Hacks: 1001 Clever Ideas to Save You Time, Money and Stress*
- *The Smart Kids Guide to Everything*
- *Create a Life You Love*
- *They Say I'm Special: 100Tips for Raising a Happy and Resilient Child with Special Needs*
- *When He's A Keeper: But You Feel like Throwing Him Away*
- *Savings Hacks: 365 Simple Ways to Keep More Money in Your Pocket*

I have found that it is easiest to write a book when I break up the material into points or chapters and work backwards to achieve my target goals.

For example, when it came to writing my *Life Hacks* book I knew that I could come up with 1001 tips. With my *Savings Hacks* book I knew that brainstorming 365 tips was an achievable goal.

My *Inspiring Teens* book included 50 important points that teens need to note to succeed in life. A few of my other books (namely: *Life Is An Experiment, Life Skills* and *They Say I'm Special* all worked with the goal of writing down 100 tips.

20,000 words divided by 100 tips is 200 words per tip. This is a simple and yet achievable goal to work towards.

As we move ahead to the brainstorming section of creating an outline or plan for your book, I want you to think about ways you can break down your content into smaller bits to work on.

It might be something like:

100 tips to achieve XYZ

50 ways you can XYZ

20 simple steps to XYZ

10 things you need to know about XYZ

You can also write:

10 chapters of 2000 words

20 chapters of 1000 words

50 chapters/tips of 400 words

100 chapters/tips of 200 words

200 chapter/tips of 100 words

I mention this to keep your mind actively thinking of ways you can break down your material so it doesn't feel so overwhelming to tackle.

There is no right or wrong way of doing this. You are the author – do what works best for you!

17. Research Is Your Best Friend

Okay so you may have noticed that we still haven't moved past the point of writing down a few ideas for your book. Well, hold your horses – this is the exact spot I want you to be right now.

If you are wondering when you will get to the writing bit, fear not...the writing is about to come!

First we need to stop and do some research. This is especially important if you plan to write a book that you want to publish and sell on Amazon or any other popular online bookstores.

I personally always do this first – before I get into the real work of writing! I imagine it is much like a builder who likes to check out other new houses that have recently been completed.

They drive around and admire other finished products. They work out what appeals to them and what doesn't. They see if there is anything that inspires them to make their own home look even better and so on.

I always make sure to first check out what else is currently published on Amazon (Amazon, in particular, because I consider them to be the biggest and best online bookstore in the world).

I do this primarily because:

a) It is useful to know your competition and
b) It can also validate whether your idea is a popular one that sells well.

Even if you are only writing your book for your personal joy and not publication, still do this step as you may see or read something that sparks an idea.

IMPORTANT TIP BEFORE YOU BEGIN!

Make sure you always have a notebook on hand (or a separate file ready to go in your Notes app on your cell phone) while you are in both "writing" and "researching" mode.

Trust me; the ideas will come to you out of nowhere and at the most random times. At midnight! Three o'clock in the morning! When you are shopping for groceries or watching a TV commercial.

Please, I beg of you: do not depend on your memory. I can't tell you how many times a great idea has floated into my head – something I thought was super important – except I was cocky and thought I would remember it later.

Only when later came, my mind was blank. Great idea, what great idea? Argh…that is a mistake you should definitely avoid making if possible.

If you are working on your laptop, start up a folder called RESEARCH. Inside this folder you can create and store a new word document called IDEAS. Copy and paste any ideas you might have straight into this file.

If you are researching using your cell phone, take screenshots of anything you would like to refer back to later. You can later transfer these screen grabs into this Research folder or use Evernote (something I will talk about more in the Writing Tools chapter)

Inside this folder I keep:

- Photos of Quotes
- Copies of books
- Website URLS
- Screen grabs
- All my notes

Or anything that I may need to refer to later!

For the record, some books require a lot of research. Other books not so much.

As for this book, I have to admit that I did zero research up until I came to this chapter. At that point I thought "oops, maybe I should check out whether anyone else has published something along the lines of *How to Publish A Non-Fiction Book in 30 Days*). Surprise, surprise, there appears to be approximately six other books with the same premise.

Now I don't want you to stress too much if a book has already been published on the same topic. If you feel that you have a **unique slant** and **something different and special to offer to this area**, it is fine to proceed with your idea.

For example, the reason I didn't baulk at the idea of writing this book (even though I discovered there are a few already published) is because I KNOW deep down that I have the life experience to offer my readers something different and special.

One of my pet hates is seeing other authors write about writing and publishing when they haven't written or published any books other than their how-to book. It irks me a lot!

As for me, I have tried and tested everything in this book many times. I practice what I preach and I don't only talk the talk, I walk the walk.

So when this idea for a non-fiction writing course started to pester me daily, I didn't feel intimidated by the other competition. To the contrary I knew I could create something unique that would possibly be even better than the rest.

When you do your own research take the time to note the following:

❖ In Amazon you can usually have a peek inside your competitor's book (see a preview or request a sample). When you do this, have a look at what the author has included in the table of contents.

- What are their chapters about? Are they writing about things that are important for you too to cover? You definitely don't want to replicate anyone's work but you need to make sure you haven't left out anything obvious.

- What works in the other books and what doesn't? What are they missing that you could include?

- Understand that all research is simply to get your own ideas flowing – not to steal content! Whatever you write about needs to be done from your own unique approach. Make sure you share your own personal take on things and offer something special.

- Do not simply regurgitate the same material that has been done a million times before, in the exact same way. BE ORIGINAL! OFFER SOMETHING UNIQUE THAT WILL EXCITE YOUR READERS!

- To help you in the research stage, think about the sort of questions your potential reader may ask. Come up with a list of 10-25 questions that they may like to have answered.

- I encourage you to be a solution provider. What is a problem that your readers are having in the real world about this topic?

How can you provide a unique solution to it? These can later form chapters or subheading headings within each chapter in your book.

- Think:

    o WHO? WHAT? WHERE?

    o WHY? HOW?

    o WHAT QUESTIONS DO I NEED TO ANSWER?

- Once again, I encourage you to make sure you keep a record of ALL YOUR RESEARCH. Keep all the books, quotes, URLS and information you may need to refer to at a later date - in the same place.

- I personally keep everything in my RESEARCH folder, only because it saves me so much time later on when I am in writing mode. When you are writing, the last thing you want to do is get distracted and lose your momentum, trying to find something that isn't obvious to find.

18. It's Time to come up with a Working Title

After all our brainstorming and research, it is time to finally commit to an idea you think might make a great book. If this idea has been crystal clear to you right from the start, I do hope some of my tips have been nonetheless helpful in laying down the foundation to your book.

Trust me; sometimes I "think" I know exactly what I want to write about. But during the process of research, the idea grows and evolves to become something even more amazing than I first expected it would be.

You may find this happens to you too. Your book may go off in tangents you don't expect. If that happens to you, go with the flow. See where it is leading you to.

SO IT'S TIME TO WRITE DOWN YOUR WORKING TITLE HERE:

....

Obviously if it's a non-fiction book, we like to also include a subtitle which is keyword-rich (we will speak about this more later). This usually clarifies to the reader exactly what your book is about. This is especially true if your 'working title' is a bit more clever and obtuse and doesn't overtly give it away.

WRITE DOWN HERE YOUR WORKING SUBTITLE:

....

Some examples of my book titles with a subtitle include:

Lightbulb Moments: 50 AHA! Insights That Will Transform Your Life

☐*Happy Thoughts: 200 Inspiring Quotes Explained for Kids and Teens*

Life Hacks: 1001 Clever Ideas to Save You Time, Money and Stress

As you can see, the subtitle helps make it quite clear to my readers exactly what my book is about. It does it in a way that the main title doesn't do on its own.

If you aren't 100% happy with the way your working title sounds right now, I don't want you to stress too much. I often change my book titles many times during the writing process, as new and better ideas come to me.

So if it doesn't sound quite right, I don't want you to worry about it! This is not the time to stop and fret about things that are not set in stone. A working title is just that – a draft idea to fuel your motivation.

I usually also create a mock up book cover too to spur me on. When I first started I would create these in Canva with a free stock photo and some fancy font. Now that I have more experience and an account with depositphotos.com, I purchase a professional photo I like. This costs only a few dollars and then I do my own mock-up in Photoshop instead.

Please note: this is never my final professional book cover. To the contrary, it serves only as a motivation for me during the writing process because I like to envision the book complete (who doesn't?). Seeing my mock book cover helps me stay on track. A bit like dangling a carrot in front of me! I want to constantly move towards that end goal.

Trust me – within a month, you too will be there.

19. Chapter Outline

Now that you have a working title and subtitle, it is time to come up with a rough plan for your book.

Sometimes this isn't easy to do from the outset, especially if you are writing your first book. But you will find it easier to develop with practice and time.

Remember, you are aiming to write only 1000 words at a time. No more and no less. To pull off this daily word count goal, it helps to have a plan or general outline to follow. Please note: this is only a GENERAL plan; it doesn't need to be too specific (unless you can and want to be).

Step 1: NOTE THE MAIN CHAPTERS

Imagine what a rough draft of your table of contents would look like. When you did the earlier Plan A exercise you would have uncovered some initial chapters to your book during the process. List them all down for me now.

Next ask yourself: what is an obvious beginning to the book? Where do you need to start? What chapters would fall into the middle and how would the book need to end?

I want you to think in the simplest terms and try to envisage a natural beginning, middle and end to your book. Come up with 10-20 chapter headings.

A minimum of 10 chapters is ideal for a 20,000 word book

Next Step: FINETUNE THE SUBHEADINGS

Each chapter can usually be broken up into few sections. I want you now to come up with a few subheadings under each chapter. List some ideas that would need to be covered, in point form.

Three to five ideas under each chapter is ideal. Not that anyone will complain if you have more!

Once again, don't stress if your ideas seems rough and amateur to start with. During the draft phase, none of your writing needs to be perfect. You simply need to get these ideas WRITTEN DOWN. If all you have is a thin outline, you can pad it out later down the track.

I promise you; those blanks won't be blank forever! You need to trust that the rest of the outline will come up naturally during the course of the month. But start with what you have! That is usually enough to get your creative juices flowing.

Timed Challenge:

In case you haven't guessed it, I love a timed challenge! I honestly think that we tap into a higher power when we are forced to think quickly and on the spot.

If the subheadings for each chapter aren't coming to you easily, I want you to pull out your timer again and give the following exercise a go.

It goes like this:

Give yourself ten minutes and TEN MINUTES ONLY to brainstorm what subheading or topics might fall under particular chapters. Write down one-liners, you don't need to go too deep here.

Once again, three to five ideas under each chapter is ideal. Not that anyone will complain if you have more!

There is only one rule when it comes to doing timed challenges. That is, you need to write down everything that comes into your mind EVEN THE CRAZY STUFF. Don't ignore the crazy ideas! My guess is that those last few wild and random thoughts that enter your mind will lead to your best work.

What to Do When Your Outline Seems Too Basic:

If you get stuck during this process, go back out and do some more research. We are so lucky to live in a day and time when the Internet is filled with a plethora of information for us to explore and read.

If there is something you need to know, research it. Keep searching for specific answers and information until you find what you need.

However a word of caution:

Try to keep the scope of your research narrow as opposed to too wide, because it is possible to get lost in a research abyss. Rather than giving you more clarity, it makes you feel more confused than ever.

Like the famous KISS acronym goes: Keep it simple, stupid!

Think about all the ingredients that will help make your book the best it can be. What would ensure it stands out from the crowd? What do you need to write about to make your book special?

Be prepared to draw on anecdotes and personal experiences when necessary. Use appropriate quotes to spur you on. Look for inspiration everywhere!

All you need to achieve by the end of this stage is this:

Brainstorm chapter ideas and write a general outline down onto paper.

Can you see any pattern emerging among your ideas? What would be the natural flow to your book?

If you haven't done so already, I encourage you to stop right now and brainstorm an initial plan that will at least get you through the first 30% of the book or 6500 words.

So if you are planning 10 chapters, I want you to come up with 3 chapters that you can begin working on straight away. If you can come up with a plan that covers more than this, woohoo! You are on a roll!

Your end goal is to have a skeleton plan that can be adapted as per your need. This initial roadmap will help get you started on your journey.

It may of course need to be adapted when any unexpected detours or exciting new destinations pop up but that will be fine! Once you have this initial plan written, we can move onto the next step.

Author's Note

I will be honest here (as I always am) and note that I have started a few books without writing a complete outline.

Yes, yes, that 30% recommendation comes from personal experience. For some books, I couldn't see the whole picture right at the beginning but I did have a brief idea of how to kick-start the projects.

Even though I didn't have a complete roadmap prepared (which would have made the writing process SO much easier) I did strongly feel like there was so much potential in my ideas.

Deep down, I knew the book ideas were worth exploring and that I could develop them further over time, with more research and dedicated thought. I knew the ideas were somewhere inside me, I just couldn't see them yet.

That is why I encourage you to work out at least 30% of your outline. It's enough to get you started and if you feel strongly about the book idea, the other 70% will come to you over time.

A WORD OF CAUTION:

If you can't come up with more than 30% of your outline right now ONLY PROCEED WITH YOUR IDEA if you are excited and passionate about the project. You need to feel like the idea will develop organically as you soon as you start writing and exploring the subject more thoroughly,

If you love the topic, I promise you the ideas and content will come!

Alternatively, if you are only half-hearted about the topic, you don't want to find after completing 30% of the book, that that was all there was to the topic. Find a topic you love, and you will work harder and stay more motivated to complete the book.

20. General 30 Day Plan

Start Date............End Date: ....

Week 1

Day 1 Monday — Write 1000 Words

Day 2 Tuesday — Write 1000 Words

Day 3 Wednesday — Write 1000 Words

Day 4 Thursday — Write 1000 Words

Day 5 Friday — Write 1000 Words

Day 6 Saturday — Rest, Relax, Revise, Brainstorm

Day 7 Sunday — Rest, Relax, Revise, Brainstorm

END WORD COUNT: 5,000 WORDS

Week 2

Day 8 Monday - Write 1000 Words

Day 9 Tuesday - Write 1000 Words

Day 10 Wednesday - Write 1000 Words

Day 11 Thursday - Write 1000 Words

Day 12 Friday - Write 1000 Words

Day 13 Saturday - Rest, Relax, Revise, Brainstorm

Day 14 Sunday - Rest, Relax, Revise, Brainstorm

END WORD COUNT: 10,000 WORDS

Week 3

Day 15 Monday - Write 1000 Words

Day 16 Tuesday - Write 1000 Words

Day 17 Wednesday - Write 1000 Words

Day 18 Thursday - Write 1000 Words

Day 19 Friday - Write 1000 Words

Day 20 Saturday - Rest, Relax, Revise, Brainstorm

Day 21 Sunday - Rest, Relax, Revise, Brainstorm

END WORD COUNT: 15,000 WORDS

Week 4

Day 22 Monday — Write 1000 Words

Day 23 Tuesday — Write 1000 Words

Day 24 Wednesday — Write 1000 Words

Day 25 Thursday — Write 1000 Words

Day 26 Friday — Write 1000 Words

Day 27 Saturday — Rest, Relax, Revise, Brainstorm

Day 28 Sunday — Rest, Relax, Revise, Brainstorm

END WORD COUNT: 20,000 WORDS

Day 29 Saturday — Edit Work / Fill in the Blanks

Day 30 Sunday — Edit Work / Fill in the Blanks

Now You Are Done – Time To Celebrate!

21 Obvious Things to Keep In Mind

- Your project doesn't have to start at the beginning or 1st of the month. You can technically begin any day you like and block out a whole 30 days for the project. For example – April 14th to May 14th or July 26th to August 26th.

- I like to start on a Monday but you can start any day of the week you like. Amend the above schedule accordingly.

- Some days you may write more than 1000 words, even when you don't have to. If that's the case, take it as a win. I like to think of it as banking extra money, which you can cash in on days when you are desperate. For example. If you are sick one day and can't write, you won't feel stressed about missing out your word count target because you already have that extra word count up your sleeve.

- Don't have any extra words up your sleeve and an emergency pops up during the week? No stress - that is what your two spare days on the weekend are for. If something causes you to miss your word count target during the week, you have the weekend to catch up to speed.

❖ For the record, procrastination is NOT an emergency. Laziness or TV is not an emergency either. I am speaking about legitimate reasons that are both unexpected and cannot be avoided. WE WANT TO AVOID THIS IF POSSIBLE.

22. Working Out When You Will Write

One of the biggest barriers that writers face is finding the time to write. Even I have struggled with this. For sure!

When I am not in my zoned-out, super-serious writing mode, I am like everyone else. I complain about the same thing – *I have no time, I'm so busy!* But here's the irony.

I still find time to check out social media every day.

I find time to watch my favourite TV shows.

I find time to answer impromptu calls from friends and have long-winded chats about nothing particularly important.

None of these things are nearly as important as my goal of writing a book and yet I still find the time to waste on these activities.

When you take on the challenge of writing a book in a month, you will need to MAKE THE TIME in your diary every day to achieve this goal.

Seriously you need to make WRITING YOUR BOOK your top priority because you somehow manage to do it for all the other important things in your life. You make the time to go to work; you keep and honour medical appointments.

This time you must MAKE THIS GOAL your most urgent priority.

OVER THE COURSE OF THE MONTH:

- ❖ You may need to cancel meetings, appointments and catch-ups with people if they aren't super urgent. Clear your calendar of all non-important events. Five hours spent socialising with friends could be five hours spent writing instead. Don't worry – you can reschedule it to next month.

- ❖ Ask for support if you need it. You can confide in your family and close friends, if you think you need to hold yourself accountable during your writing month.

- ❖ Don't be afraid to tell people the truth. You are working on an important project. You plan to write a book in one month. If people are offended when you cancel your plans with them, try not to care so much. Being offended is their choice and their problem; not yours.

- ❖ Make sure you time this book-writing project well. You don't want to start it when you have a major work deadline or a million other things looming over your head. Try to choose a time in your schedule when it is less intense but not necessarily quiet. If you are waiting for a totally quiet diary that day will never come!

- ❖ For the record I personally jump in and start researching and writing straight away when I get an idea. I've written books during all sorts of circumstances – including the crazier, more hectic months.

- ❖ For example, when my son was in hospital having surgery and recuperating for five weeks, I wrote from his bedside, even though I was surviving on next to no sleep. I've also written books in the lead up to Christmas, while working full-time, freelancing with a heavy workload, and even during school holidays (in case you don't know, young kids at home every day = zero free time for mom).

- ❖ Be flexible with the word count. Don't try to force out any more words than is necessary to complete the purpose of your book. You may come to 18,000 words and not be able to squeeze out another word. If that's the case, it is okay to stop there if you consider that your book is complete at that point.

- ❖ Or you may reach 20,000 words and think there are still some topics that you need to address. If that happens to you, keep on writing. Just because I work with a 20,000 word goal, doesn't mean you can't write 24,000 or 27,000 words. Yes, it may take a few more days but you need to do whatever it takes to make your book feel like it has covered everything that needs to be covered.

- ❖ It helps immensely to know what your purpose is in advance. Who are you writing this book for? Be specific about your target audience. What you are hoping for them to get from your book? You need to summarise this information in one or two sentences. Once you have defined your purpose and objective, print it out and keep it in front of you to refer back to at all times.

23. Create a Writing Schedule

Once you have cleared your calendar, you need to work out when you write most effectively. Are you a morning person or a night person? Does it suit you to write before everyone else has woken up or after everyone has gone to bed?

Can you take notes during the day and sneak in some writing whenever you get a break? Or do you work better when you set aside a large chunk of time for the job?

When I worked full-time and still managed to write 1,000 words a day, I would wake up early to write down my initial ideas for the day. During the course of the day I would scribble down more ideas if they came to mind. Then the moment I came home, I would set aside an hour or two for writing and pull everything together.

When I was a mom of two young kids (a baby and toddler) I would wait until both children were put to bed and write every night from 7:30-9:30 (after that I would crash out because I was so exhausted).

The first thing you need to do is decide when you have some free time. If everyone wakes up at 7am, you can possibly squeeze in two hours of writing from 5am-7am.

If you travel by public transport to get to work, you could maybe write your words on the way there and back home at night. If you used to watch TV after dinner, you can maybe now use this time instead to write.

If it isn't obvious to you straight away where you can fit in your writing, you need to be a lot more brutal with the time you have. Analyse everything that is currently filling up your schedule.

Remember, we all have the same 24 hours to use every day. Whether you are the president of a country or CEO of a company or Oprah, we each have 1440 minutes or 86,400 seconds to take advantage of every day. Your goal is to use your share wisely.

Study what activities currently fill up your day. If you spend an hour cooking dinner every night, could you perhaps order takeaway instead or organise the simplest meals for the month (tuna on rice, eggs on toast, grilled chicken and meat – trust me, no one will die if you serve them basic food instead of complicated gourmet meals for a short while).

Can you get your family to help you out with the household chores? Can they take care of themselves for a change? If you have young kids, can they watch a movie or two during the day to give you some more free time?

If you have to take your older kids to activities, can you bring your laptop with you and do your writing in the car? Can you book in a cleaner or babysitter to take care of some of the more stressful jobs you have on your plate?

Say no to all the unnecessary activities and most important of all:

Now is the time for you to call in all your favours!

Be firm with your commitment to writing. No-one questions a surgeon who has to cancel a dinner to go perform emergency surgery or a tradesman who has an urgent callout to attend.

Give yourself the same privilege of taking the time to do something that is important to you. You don't have to explain yourself; you don't have to make excuses or feel guilty. All you need to do is find the time to write and do whatever you can to find that time!

24. Find a Good Writing Environment

I'll tell you what I am pretty sure won't make for a great working environment:

- Having the TV or radio on while you write
- Having lots of distractions around you
- Having people constantly interrupt you
- Keeping your phone on loud as opposed to silent

If you plan to make the time to write (which of course you will), you need to work out WHERE you do your best work because that will lead to higher productivity.

Now I have personally found lots of different places have worked for me, at different stages of my life. When I write early in the morning or late at night, I usually write IN BED, snuggled under the blankets, with the laptop on my lap.

This works especially well for me in the mornings as my husband wakes up super early for work. When he gets up at 5 in the morning, I get up too! At night however it's a different story, as he goes to sleep way earlier than me, so I write in the guest room.

I love both these writing times as the house is SO QUIET because the kids are both asleep! Win, win!

As for *during the day*, lately I have found writing at home next to impossible, even when I have a day off, even when the kids are both at school! This is because I get super distracted when I am home alone.

I see other things that need to be done – there's always cleaning, washing and organising to do around the house. Or I go into the kitchen and think I should start prepping dinner early etcetera. Honestly the chores are ALWAYS there – I can't escape it no matter how hard I try. It's a horrid cycle that never ends and simply repeats itself every week without fail!

Thankfully I have found a solution to this. I now go to the library during my designated writing days or whenever I have some free time.

Our local library is amazing. It offers free Wi-Fi, comfortable working spaces, and most important of all, peace and quiet. (Added bonus: all the books provide me with so much inspiration!)

It took me a day or two to get used to this new environment but now I zone out and go straight into writing mode when I am there. It is my go-to place if I have missed writing in the morning or have plans for the night and need to squeeze in some productive time.

If you don't have this option available I want to assure you that in the past, I have written thousands and thousands of words in some of the weirdest locations. I used to love writing in my car, sitting there with my car-seat pushed all the way back and immersed in my book within this strange little bubble.

I used to also love writing in the backyard, sprawled across a picnic blanket or on my couch at home, with my headphones on, listening to nature music playing in the background (I love the sound of birds chirping, gentle water flowing and trees rustling!)

There is no right or wrong place for you to write. You need to find what works best for YOU. Test out different spots until you find something that seems to make you write and work more productively. Once you have a preferred spot, stick with it until you feel like you need to change it or shake things up.

For the record, you do not have to have a designated room like an office or study to be a productive writer. I have written 18 books, without ever sitting down at a writing desk! Yes it's true!

Up until recently (a few months ago) I didn't even have a designated workspace at home (remember I mentioned I loved writing in bed!). When I did create one, it ended up in my kid's large playroom so I could attend to work and personal emails and other blog stuff right there near my children while they kept themselves busy with more fun stuff. So not having a private desk, office or study shouldn't deter you from writing.

Your goal is simple: pick a spot where you feel:

- ❖ Comfortable
- ❖ You have some privacy and quiet and finally
- ❖ It contributes and leads to your highest productivity.

25. Make Sure You Regularly Back Up Your Work

Before we talk about the process of writing itself, I want to stop and make sure you understand how important it is that you regularly back up your work.

> I cannot stress to you how important this point is!

You will need to back up your writing every day on your computer and also to a USB.

Back it up to two USBs if you can!

Plus you can also save it to a free online storage account like Dropbox, OneDrive or Google Drive. It is free to start a basic account so take advantage of this fact. This gives you the added benefit of being able to access your work anywhere where there is Internet.

If it sounds like I am going over the top with this point, I promise you there is a good reason for it.

It is almost a rite of passage for writers to lose their work. I can't even begin to tell you how gut-wrenching it feels to start your work again.

Save yourself this headache and make sure you are regularly backing up your work.

To do this in Microsoft Word:

- Go To FILE
- Then OPTIONS
- Under OPTIONS go to SAVE
- Under Auto-Recover make it auto-save the document EVERY 5 MINUTES.

In the instance of writing, it is better to be safe than sorry.

26. Okay I Have My Plan — So How Do I Start Writing?

When it comes to writing a book, there is only so much research and preparation you can do before you have no choice but to jump right in and write.

Remember to be a writer, you need to write.

I think what stalls a lot of writers is this: they think they have to write in the order of the book. Plus they think that everything has to be written perfectly the first time, which couldn't be further from the truth.

The first draft of anything always needs additional editing and revision. Remember, you are not at that end-stage yet! You need to get some words onto paper first!

I encourage you to start wherever you want to begin. If you have a favourite, easy or short chapter, start there! You can start in the middle of the book or write an introduction to some of your chapter headings.

I usually go with my favourite chapters first. Because my chapters are always short and sweet, I get so much satisfaction from finishing one and moving onto the next chapter. I like to work on one idea at a time and don't worry so much about how it will all fall into place at the end.

As time goes on, you will see a natural order appear in your work. With some books, I was constantly moving chapter ideas around until right at the end when I knew and understood the material a lot better. Only then could I imagine what would make most sense to the reader.

Note: some days your writing may seem terrible. You may think it totally sucks and want to throw in the towel. Even still, you need to keep writing and not give up! The only way you will improve is if you stick with writing, day in and day out. You will get better with practice, I promise you, if you adhere to our 1,000 words a day plan.

How? Well, it is consistency that makes creativity easier for a writer. Over time, the words will come to you easier and you will be able to write faster too. You will be truly inspired NOT BEFORE you sit down to start your book but after you see your words on paper.

Once again, as John Dufresne said,

"The purpose of the first draft is not to get it right, but to get it written."

Simply get it written! That is your goal - 1,000 words x 20 days!

I request that you don't edit your writing as you go (at least not before you have completed your 1000 words for the day). You can come back and do that later if you like or have the time (use your weekends for this revision).

Why? Because it is a mistake to sit there and criticise every word you write when you are in your writing mode. This high level criticism will only make you feel more frustrated, stressed and anxious.

ON YOUR WRITING DAYS, YOU ARE A WRITER NOT AN EDITOR!

You can try to get your words perfect once your manuscript is complete – that's what all the later drafts are for.

Remember, your book won't write itself. You need to put pen to paper or fingers to the keyboard to make that happen.

Stick with the goal, even when you don't feel like doing it. Even if you aren't sure if you are doing a good job or not - rain, hail or shine, I want you to show up and make your dream of completing this book come true.

WRITE.

WRITE.

WRITE.

WRITE.

WRITE.

27. Find Your Voice

If you are lucky, you will find and embrace your writing voice immediately. But for some people, this is what gets in the way of their productivity.

They write in a style that doesn't come naturally to them.

They allow their expectations of how their writing "should" sound to get in the way of their own writing.

This leads to them feeling unsatisfied and disconnected from their writing because it doesn't feel honest and authentic to them.

Finding your writing voice can take time to learn and develop but I encourage you to do this.

This will make the writing process so much easier for you! Whatever your voice may be – casual, conversational, proper, professional, light-hearted or serious, go with it! You have your own style – you don't have to try to copy someone else's.

28. When You Get Stuck For Ideas

Ah the dreaded writer's block. No need to fret!

Here are some tips that you can use when you get stuck for ideas and/or need to kick that stupid block to the kerb:

- ❖ Always keep your audience in mind. What questions are they looking to have answered? What are they hoping to read and find in your book?

- ❖ If it's boring to you, it will probably be boring to your reader. If you are feeling bored, lost or confused about your writing, try to find a different more fun and exciting way to present your content. There's always a way to mix things up and provide a unique twist to your material. You need to open your mind to finding it.

- For example, write a few Top 10 or Fun Facts lists. Ask simple mock-up questions from the viewpoint of the reader and provide the answers (like the popular DEAR ABBY column). See if you can come up with a new approach to your ideas.

- Give real life examples. Share stories to back up your information.

- Jot down the most basic points – only the bare bones - to get your point across. You can come back to it later, to flesh it out and fill in the details.

- Don't be afraid to jump around. If you are stuck, move around to something different. You can come back to this part later when you have more clarity on the idea.

- Look for inspiration everywhere. Search online for ideas or pull out any old books you may own on the topic. Inspiration can be found in the strangest places.

- Ask yourself "what would be the next obvious step in the story I am telling? What would keep the flow moving forward? Focus on this and nothing else if you are stuck! What do you need to write next?

- If you are truly stuck, take a break and read. Watch how other writers weave their content together in their own books. Are they doing something you would like to replicate? Writers can learn a lot from reading often and studying how effective writing is done.

- Force yourself to shake off your writer's block. It can help if you remind yourself to stop being so precious about your writing. Get over your perfectionist tendencies and write whatever comes to mind. Seriously, keep writing, even if it is only in your journal.

- Instead of taking a break, persist even when you are feeling stuck. Sit down and write 100 words (even if you don't feel like it). Then write another 100 words (it can be about something unrelated). Start small, write in very small blocks. Do this several times a day.

- Try writing about something totally random to get your creative juices flowing again. Maybe it can be a story from your childhood or teenage years. Perhaps it can be about your greatest accomplishments and biggest fears. Even if you don't ever use it in your book, I still want you to write it. Because the more you write, no matter what you are writing about, the better you will get at it. Here's a simple <u>RANDOM WRITING PROMPTS GENERATOR</u> to check out for ideas.

- ❖ Give yourself permission to be terrible. So what if you haven't quite mastered the art of writing eloquently! You can go back and fix everything later when you are in the editing phase.

- ❖ See my USEFUL WRITING TOOLS chapters for more tools that may help break you out of your funk. The ones I think may be useful are <u>PORTENT'S CONTENT IDEA GENERATOR</u> and <u>SOOLVE</u>.

29. Other Writing Tips

- Celebrate your achievements and reward yourself for the hard work you have done so far. Even the small wins are something special to treasure. Think of it this way: once you write 1000 words, you are 5% there. Once you finish 2000 words, you are 10% there and 3000 words = 15% complete. It is all about taking small, consistent, baby steps.

- Remember, feeling negative or stressed about the writing process isn't going to help you in any way. Revisit the earlier chapter on fear, when I spoke about how challenges are impossible to avoid during your writing month. **They will come up,** I promise you. So be prepared rather than surprised, when they show up.

- Read your writing out loud. Does it sound natural or stilted? If so, make the appropriate changes.

- Keep a journal. You can note here what is and isn't working for you during the writing phase. If you need to vent, vent out onto paper and see if any answers come to you during the process.

- I always, always, keep a journal when I am writing so I can track my goals and feelings about the project. Writing in my journal feels like I'm confiding in a best friend, without any judgement attached.

- Always have your notebook and pen handy so you can jot down notes for your book when your ideas pop up at the most unexpected times. Keep one on your bedside table, work desk, in your car, bag and kitchen etcetera. Refer to these notes whenever you get stuck.

- Make a list of your key or trigger words that are important to your book. Remember I mentioned this when you were coming up with the subtitle for your book? Keywords are words that are searchable within Google and Amazon and tie in with the theme for your book.

- An example of some of my key trigger words for my parenting books include: *positive parenting, parenting advice, helping children succeed and raising great kids*. These key trigger words help encapsulate exactly what my book is about. They remind me what I am hoping to achieve. Do the same with your book and refer to them often when you feel like you are going off track.

- ❖ Can you describe your book in a sentence? Or even better, come up with a sales pitch or the essence of the book in ten words or less. I challenged myself to do the same for all 18 of my books, which was difficult but eye-opening. Do the same for your book if you can.

- ❖ It is also important that you take care of yourself during your writing month. When you feel healthy and great, it leads to better work and higher productivity. Eat well, go for a walk when you need a break, cut out the junk, drink lots of water and make sure you get lots of rest.

- ❖ It is a simple suggestion but TRUST ME, self-care is essential when you are working as hard as you are planning to work during this month. Be selfish for a change and put yourself first, instead of prioritising your needs behind everyone else's.

30. Avoid These Top 5 Writing Mistakes

1. Don't over-explain things. Some writers go on and on about things, assuming the reader needs to know every little step in their process of thinking but that isn't the case.

2. Get rid of needless words. You can remove most of these words without making any difference to your writing (keep it only if the sentence seems weird without it).

The most popular culprits include:

- REALLY
- VERY
- JUST
- THEN
- TOTALLY
- COMPLETELY

- ABSOLUTELY
- LITERALLY
- DEFINITELY
- CERTAINLY
- PROBABLY
- ACTUALLY
- BASICALLY
- VIRTUALLY
- RATHER
- SOMEWHAT
- SOMEHOW

3. Remember the writer's rule: show, don't tell. Show your readers how something might look in action; don't only teach them the principles.

4. Don't leave your reader hanging. Tell them what they need to know now.

5. Ensure correct grammar and spelling. I know it's human to make mistakes (I make them often, due to the speed I write).

   However do your best to eliminate these annoying errors from your final manuscript. P.S. If you find any within this book, please let me know!

31. Get Some Support from Fellow Writers

Writing sometimes feels like a solitary, lonely job. You can often get stuck inside your own head or feel like you don't have anyone to turn to for support or to help you get over writer's block (which we will talk more about later.)

To help you get over this, I recommend that you can join a few Facebook writing groups. Here is a list of 20 groups that you may find valuable:

<u>Australian Women Who Write</u>

<u>The Write Life Community</u>

<u>Write, Promote and Sell Books</u>

<u>Writers Group</u>

<u>Authors</u>

<u>Young Australian Writers</u>

<u>Guerrilla Publishing</u>

[Authors Working Together](#)

[Pat's First Kindle Book](#)

[Indie Author Group](#)

[Write On! Online](#)

[Writers Helping Writers](#)

[NaNoWriMo Participants](#)

[Create If Writing](#)

[Writer's Next Step](#)

[The Copywriter Club](#)

[Writing Revolters](#)

Please feel free to join any groups that appeal to you. At the time of writing, some groups are more active than others. That's not to say they don't offer valuable advice in their previous posts.

If you don't feel comfortable posting your writing woes, look through what others have shared in the past. You may find someone has already spoken about similar struggles and sought support from the group.

Seek inspiration and guidance from all the great tips other people share within these groups. That is the quickest way to learn – from other people's mistakes.

32. Useful Writing Tools

Here are some tools that may help you during the writing process:

The Freebies

You don't need to spend anything to start enjoying these today.

DAILY PAGE

Sign up here to receive a new writing prompt every day.

GOOGLE DOCS

Google Docs can be used in lots of different ways to improve your writing. You can use it to request edits or comments from your peers. It will also store your research and writing drafts in a cloud-based file. It even has a built-in dictionary if you ever need it.

PORTENT'S CONTENT IDEA GENERATOR

This little tool is great when you are feeling stuck for ideas. You can enter any subject you like into the generator and it will come up with some weird and wacky suggestions. Keep hitting refreshing if you would like to see some more alternative ideas.

SOOLVE

I love Soolve! All you need to do here is type any keyword into the box and it will automatically search for the most popular terms across numerous search engines. If the terms are popular, it means people are interesting in knowing more about it.

READABILITY TEST TOOL

The Readability Test Tool will provide you with a quick and easy way to test the readability of your work. Even though it's commonly used to test web pages, you can also type or copy your text straight into the direct input box. If you need to keep your work simple (and not complicated) this is a free way to test the reading and age level that your writing can be understood from.

VOICE DICTATION APPS

If your thoughts run faster than your fingers do, considering having your work transcribed. Some people find they prefer speaking out their ideas in the initial stages of their project, instead of writing them down.

If that's the case, consider downloading a free dictation application from the App Store. You can use your voice to dictate your notes and the text will simply appear. Dragon Dictation is a popular paid one but there are plenty of free options available on the market too.

EVERNOTE

Evernote is a free app that is designed for note taking, organising and archiving. It is a FABULOUS tool for writer. It allows you to collect texts, screenshots, photos, voice memos and more and organise them with tags and folders so you never lose anything.

The premium version of the app also syncs across all your devices – on your computer, via a web browser and on a smartphone app – so you always have access to EVERYTHING. Cost is $9.99 a month but it is fine to stick to the free version of this like I do.

QUORA

If you have a random question about anything, you can be sure to find the answer here. Otherwise, ask a question yourself and wait to see who responds.

The $$ Tools

No writing book would be complete without mentioning the three most popular paid writing tools – GRAMMARLY, HEMINGWAY APP and SCRIVENER. I mention them only so that you know that they are legitimate tools that come highly recommended. In fact, they are considered to be the best of the best!

GRAMMARLY

Grammarly is a robust, sophisticated program that automatically detects grammar, spelling, punctuation, word choice, and style mistakes in your writing. There is a free option available, which identifies spelling and grammatical errors (in a more detailed way than MS Word).

However the paid premium version, which costs $29.95 a month, takes it to a completely different level. Only look into this software if you think you require additional assistance in your writing and editing.

HEMINGWAY APP

Like Grammarly above, the goal of Hemingway App is to make your writing bold and clear. I have only recently purchased it and have to say, I understand now why so many people rave about this software.

The app is great for analysing your text in the following ways:

Anything marked in **YELLOW**: highlights lengthy, complex sentences and common errors. If you see a yellow sentence, it recommends you shorten or split it.

Anything marked in **RED** highlights a sentence that is so dense and complicated that your readers will get lost trying to follow it. It recommends that you edit the sentence to remove the red.

Super long words are marked in **PURPLE**. You can utilize a shorter word in place of anything highlighted in PURPLE. If you mouse over the word it will even offer you some hints!

Anything marked in **BLUE** notes an adverb and weakening phrases – it is recommended that you get rid of these and pick words with more force.

Anything marked in **GREEN** notes phrases or sentences that use a passive voice.

Simply paste in some of your work into this app and edit away. Or, click the Write button and compose something new. (Please note: this app now costs $19.99 and is not essential to get you started).

SCRIVENER

If we are chatting about writing tools, the final must-mention is Scrivener. This software is the go-to app for writers of all kinds, used every day by best-selling novelists, screenwriters, non-fiction writers, students, journalists and more.

My honest review: I am old-fashioned and like to type straight into MS Word, the same way I have been writing for 20 years.

However I still bought Scrivener because I was intrigued by all the features it offers writers. It takes a while to get your head around how amazing and advanced this software is – your mind will truly boggle at all the things it offers like:

- The binder section to keep any related documents together and organised

- The ability to colour-code your documents by whatever data you want to track

- The different views —like the virtual cork board where you can view each document as an index card and move things around

- The goal setting tools whereby you can set word count goals and track your progress.

- You can import research documents, web pages and links and photos right into your project

And there is so much more! This writing tool is as fancy as it gets. My only recommendation is that you take the time to watch some videos on how to utilise it properly otherwise you may miss some of the more advanced features. Cost is $40 for Windows and $45 for the Mac Version.

After Note:

Here's the truth. You don't need to spend **any** money on writing tools to complete your non-fiction book in 30 days. In fact, none of these tools were even invented back when I first started writing (no Internet, no nothing!) You can achieve your goal of 20,000 words without utilising any of these tools.

If however you are one of those people who like to get new running shoes before you jump into an exercise regime or you want to have backup, go for it! Do whatever it takes and use whatever tools you think will help you get to the end goal.

But remember this: these tools WON'T do the writing for you. You still need to DO THE WORK, day in, day out. There's no secret, magic recipe to writing unless you count DISCIPLINE and CONSISTENCY as the essential ingredients.

33. Summarizing the Most Important Points

Here are the ten top tips you need to follow to succeed in completing your non-fiction book within 30 days:

1. Decide what your book will be about.
2. Write an outline.
3. Achieve your daily word count – 1000 words.
4. Write one chapter at a time.
5. Choose a comfortable spot to write.
6. MAKE the time to write, preferably when you have little distractions.
7. Let go of your need for perfection.
8. Save editing for weekends – your goal is to write, not edit yet.
9. Stay motivated – you CAN and will do it!
10. Celebrate your win when you are done – you deserve it!

34. Writing Quotes To Spur You On

To download your two bonus books, which collectively include a total of 200 writing quotes, visit the following link. They should keep you inspired during your darker days.

http://www.inspiringlifedreams.com/free-stuff/

35. In Conclusion

So we have now reached the end of this book and the beginning of your new adventure. In your hands you hold a useful step-by-step blueprint to help you write a 20,000 word non-fiction book in 30 days.

You now have all the information required to help you achieve this goal. You know what you need to do. You know how to do it.

All that is missing is the final step: ACTION. I have total faith that you can do it.

The only thing standing in your way between you and your book is 30 days of consistent work.

There is no reason why you can't go off and write that amazing book right now. You know you can do it! The book is living inside you and dying to get out so set it free.

No more excuses. It's time to take action. Your time is now.

You know you want it so be courageous. Step outside your comfort zone, take a deep breath and begin writing, one word at a time.

I wish you the best of luck on your writing journey.

Stay In Touch

If you ever have any questions or would like to share your success stories with me, please feel free to email me on:

inspiringlifedreams@outlook.com

Alternatively you can find me blogging and spilling my heart at:

www.inspiringlifedreams.com

Frances Vidakovic

My Books

Fiction

- *Just A Little Break*
- *Pretty Mansnatchers*
- *Before I Die*
- *Enchanted Island*
- *Until I Fall Again*

Non-Fiction

- *Boost Your Blog Traffic – 50 Strategic Steps To Increase Traffic To Your Blog and Make It A Success (Available only via www.inspiringlifedreams.com)*
- *Do Something!: The No-BS Guide For Anyone Who Needs To Stop Wasting Their Time Today*

- *Inspiring Teens: A Guide To Living Life Without Regret*

- *Life Is An Experiment: 100 Experiments To Change Your Life*

- *Life Skills: 100 Things Every Kid Needs To Know Before Leaving Home*

- *Lightbulb Moments: 50 AHA! Insights That Will Transform Your Life*

- *Happy Thoughts: 200 Inspiring Quotes Explained for Kids and Teens*

- *Life Hacks: 1001 Clever Ideas To Save You Time, Money and Stress*

- *The Smart Kids Guide to Everything*

- *Create a Life You Love*

- *They Say I'm Special: 100Tips for Raising a Happy and Resilient Child with Special Needs*

- *When He's A Keeper: But You Feel Like Throwing Him Away*

- *Savings Hacks: 365 Simple Ways To Keep More Money In Your Pocket*

- *Croatian Princess – Confessions From A Croatian-Born Australian and Her Life Back Home*

Printed in Great Britain
by Amazon